Some facets of the UK you will not
have seen

BRITAIN IN OLD PHOTOGRAPHS

SALFORD

EDWARD GRA

In friendship
Sharon Brearley

Budding
BOOKS

This book was first published in 1995 by
Alan Sutton Publishing, an imprint of
Sutton Publiahing Limited

This edition first published in 2001 by
Budding Books, an imprint of
Sutton Publishing Limited

Copyright © Edward Gray, 1995

British Library Cataloguing in Publication Data.
A catalogue record for this book is available from
the British Library.

ISBN 1 84015 184 6

Typeset in 9/10 Sabon.
Typesetting and origination by
Sutton Publishing Limited.
Printed in Great Britain by
J.H. Haynes & Co. Ltd, Sparkford.

Contents

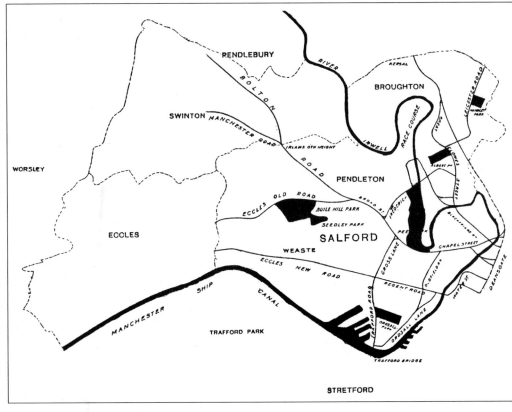

Main roads in Salford, Pendleton, and Broughton, 1900–30.

Introduction

The present City of Salford was created in 1974, when local government reorganisation extended the former boundaries to incorporate the districts of Eccles, Irlam, Swinton & Pendlebury, and Worsley. However, for the purpose of this book, the Salford depicted is that of pre-1974 vintage, and the aforementioned districts have been excluded.

The former County Borough of Salford, which was accorded the status of a city in 1926, was itself a creation of an earlier boundary extension in 1853, by which the adjoining settlements of Pendleton and Broughton were merged with the older Salford.

The original ancient settlement lay within a curve of the River Irwell, and the name Salford is thought to derive from the Old English word 'Sahl' (for sallow, or willow), the full name meaning 'the ford by the willow'. In Anglo-Saxon times Lancashire was divided into areas known as 'hundreds', and the 1086 Domesday Book records that the land in the south-east corner was known as the 'Hundred of Salford', a subordinate manor being that of Manchester. The title 'hundred' was conferred on an area from which the monarch might expect a hundred families to provide a hundred men to fight his wars. A 'hundred' was also the basic unit for raising taxes. In those sparsely populated times, the number of people in the whole of the Hundred of Salford would have been a mere 3,000, of which total Salford, Pendleton and Broughton would account for only a small proportion.

Salford began to emerge as a small town in the thirteenth century, having its own weekly market and annual fair. It was granted a Charter as a Free Borough in 1230, the new status conferring certain rights for its citizens, regulating and promoting trade, and permitting the town to hold its own law court. The Salford Charter became the model for later grants to Stockport and Manchester, and remained the basis of the town's government for over 500 years.

Wool and flax were the fibres used in the early textile trade, cotton becoming important only after the mid-1600s. Moving from the home-based cottage industries, weavers and spinners began to be employed in workshops and warehouses attached to the homes of merchants. Goods were sold at fairs and markets, and some of the leading merchants traded through London. The growth of trade, and the problems of transporting raw materials and finished goods, led to the development of better means of communication. By 1736 the rivers Mersey and Irwell had been dredged and widened so that boats could sail from the Mersey estuary to the warehouses of Salford Quay, then located between Chapel Street and the river.

Unfortunately, the river navigation had a number of disadvantages. Its course was long and winding, and droughts or floods sometimes made it unusable. In 1759 the Duke of Bridgewater began his pioneering canal enterprise to transport coal from his Worsley mines to Salford. By 1773 the Duke's canal had been extended to Runcorn, offering a more reliable waterway to the sea, and competing with the river navigation for both goods and passengers. Another canal, linking Manchester, Bolton and Bury, was open by 1796. Its course ran through Salford, and its terminal wharves were at Oldfield Road. Coal from mines at Pendleton and Agecroft was the principal traffic, some of the pit-heads being so close to the waterway that coal could be transferred direct into waiting barges. The canal also provided a source of water for many of the industries which grew up along its banks. In 1835 there was even a small brewery near Windsor Bridge which took its water for brewing from the canal! The canal also offered a packet-boat service for parcels and passengers between Salford and Bolton. Later, a connection was made to the river navigation via a series of six locks near Oldfield Road.

More favourable conditions for the transport of goods by road in horse-drawn wagons had meantime been achieved by the creation of a turnpike system. In 1753 the Pendleton Turnpike Trust had gained powers to 'turnpike' three roads spreading fan-wise from Salford, and leading to Warrington (for Liverpool), Chorley, and Bolton. In return for the Trust's investment in improving the road surfaces, tolls were charged to commercial users at bars (turnpikes) erected at intervals along the highway. In 1754, the road through Broughton connecting Manchester and Bury (Bury Old Road) was similarly improved, and others followed.

The district's first railway came in 1830, when the Liverpool & Manchester line passed through Salford. At first intended for goods rather than passengers, the motive for railway construction was the same as had inspired the river and canal enterprises and the road improvements – namely the urgent need for the more efficient carriage of raw materials and manufactured goods. Such was the confidence in this new form of transport, that in 1831 the proprietors of the Manchester, Bolton & Bury Canal added the words 'And Railway' to the Company title, and gained powers to build a railway on the line of the canal. Aiming to close the canal entirely, the Company eventually bowed to pressure from coal-owners who did not want to lose access to cheap water transport, and the new railway was opened in 1838 alongside the canal, following its course closely through Salford. By the end of the century, the area had a close network of industrial and passenger railways.

Throughout the nineteenth century, industry had continued to expand and diversify. Bleachers, dyers, calico printers, and machine-makers served the textile trade. Soap manufacturers supplied both the textile and domestic markets. New industries, such as engineering and machine tool making, became established. Salford boasted the first factory to be lit entirely by gas (Phillips & Lee, 1806), and as early as 1850 electric lighting had been demonstrated at Pendleton. Indeed, in the second half of the century, the manufacture of wires, cables, switchgear, and components for the new electrical industry dominated developments.

The dissatisfaction of traders with railway freight rates, and the high dues charged on goods shipped through the Port of Liverpool, resulted in the construction of the Manchester Ship Canal, which enabled ocean-going vessels to load and discharge their cargoes closer to the region's factories. The terminal docks in Salford gave a further boost to local industry and employment prospects in 1894.

A century earlier, it had been calculated that Salford, Pendleton, and Broughton combined had some 7,000 inhabitants. This total had increased dramatically as steam-powered factories had taken the place of the former home industries. By 1900 the population had grown to 220,000. The rapid scale of this increase was hardly exceeded in other parts of the country, and an unfortunate result in the Victorian period was the creation of vast areas of poor-quality back-to-back terraced housing, much of which was not replaced until the mid-twentieth century.

Today, the old staple industries have vanished, but some former cotton mills are home to a variety of new trades. The decline of manufacturing industry has been matched by a diminishing use of the Ship Canal, though the old docklands now have prestigious new developments. Reconstruction and re-planning since the 1950s has changed the face of the old city, and the population has fallen as Salfordians have moved to outer suburbs.

Section One

THE TOWNSHIP OF SALFORD

Of the three townships which made up the 1853 borough, Salford became the most densely populated and the most heavily industrialised. In the mid-1700s, the buildings of the old town were concentrated mainly in the Greengate and Chapel Street area, close to the bridge over the river to Manchester but, as trade and industry advanced, further development took place along the lines of the main roads radiating from Manchester. The boundary with Pendleton was reached at a spot close to Cross Lane, on the busy highway which carried traffic between Manchester and Liverpool.

In the Victorian period, the continued growth of trade and commerce, coupled with the rapid rise in the number of town dwellers, resulted in the construction of high density housing mixed with assorted industrial buildings, wherever vacant plots of land could be found. Since the 1950s much reconstruction and redevelopment has taken place, removing much of the old terraced housing, but creating a new blight in the form of high-rise flats, and bisecting the city with motorways and trunk roads designed to speed people through the city as rapidly as possible.

Chapel Street, Salford

The principal road linking Salford with Manchester is Chapel Street. Always a busy thoroughfare, it had seen the town's first omnibus service in 1824, horse-trams in 1877, and in 1901 was one of the first roads chosen for conversion to the electric tramway system. Because residents objected to the unsightly overhead wires, the Tramways Department countered criticism by adorning the centre poles with ornamental bases, wrought-iron work, and decorative finials. Prominent in this 1905 view (looking towards Manchester, from the corner of Oldfield Road) is the spire of St John's Roman Catholic Cathedral. Further away is the spire of a Presbyterian church, which stood at the corner of St Stephen Street. The spire was dismantled when the church was converted to a cinema in 1913. In recent years the building has returned to its former use as a chapel. Nearby, the old Salford Town Hall, built in 1844 in Bexley Square, remains in use today as a Magistrates' Court. Chapel Street was the setting for Henry Hobson's High Class Boot & Shoe Emporium in Harold Brighouse's play *Hobson's Choice*. The apprentice, Will Mossop, competed from a rented cellar round the corner in the less salubrious Oldfield Road. (Valentine)

The Crescent, Salford, 1935. A continuation of Chapel Street, the main road (right) follows the meander of the River Irwell. In the middle distance is Salford Royal Hospital, with the tower of St Philip's Church and the Cathedral spire beyond. (A.H. Clarke)

Cross Lane, Salford, 1902. Formerly a country lane, the road became an important link to the docks after the opening of the Ship Canal in 1894. The flag flies proudly from the castellated frontage of the barracks, home to the 7th and 8th Battalions, Lancashire Fusiliers. (Goddard)

Regent Road, viewed from Eccles New Road, at the junction with Cross Lane and Trafford Road, *c.* 1925. Before the installation of automatic signals, traffic at this busy intersection was controlled by a policeman wearing a white coat and helmet. (C. Wilkinson)

Regent Road developed on the line of a second turnpike road to Eccles after the construction of Regent Bridge in 1808. Once an important shopping centre, nothing now remains to identify this 1907 view, which looks towards the junction with Oldfield Road. The 1892 Public Baths appear on the right. Notice the carcasses hanging outside the butcher's shop on the left. (C. Wilkinson)

Regent Road, looking towards Regent Bridge, in August 1939. A branch of the National Westminster Bank stands on the corner of Oldfield Road. In the far distance looms the bulk of the Dominion Cinema. The tramcar is working on the docks circular route. (WAC)

Trafford Road, *c.* 1910. This was the main artery for traffic to and from the docks. Viewed at its upper end, towards the Cross Lane junction, the Clowes Hotel (much frequented by sailors) is on the left, with the spire of Stowell Memorial Church (presently retained as a landmark) in the distance. (JLB)

At the corner of New Park Road and Trafford Road, opposite the main dock entrance, stood a police and fire station, which was also the original Custom House. A new building, further along Trafford Road, replaced it in the late 1890s. A third Custom House was constructed in 1970. This photograph was taken in about 1904. (C. Wilkinson)

The docks and the industries of Trafford Park created much traffic along Trafford Road. In peak hours, tramcars carried thousands of workers to and from the Trafford Bridge terminus, which was in an unprepossessing side street – Ordsall Lane, seen here in 1939. (D. Rourke)

Section Two

PENDLETON

Until 1853 Pendleton was, like Broughton, a separate township. Though situated on the same side of the river as Salford, it had more in common with Broughton, and joined the municipal borough with reluctance. As with Broughton, Pendleton's inhabitants were fewer and generally wealthier than those of Salford, and the district was regarded as a desirable residential area for Manchester businessmen who wished to live out of town. The road through Pendleton to Eccles was known for many years as 'Millionaire's Row' because of its large number of great houses, one of which was the residence of a Lord Mayor of Manchester.

Industrial development, when it came, was located away from the rich residential areas, and was sited mainly along the line of the Irwell Valley.

Lying at the junction of two main routes, where the road from Liverpool met that from Bolton, Chorley, and the north, Pendleton was an important stage on the way to Manchester. In 1824 a Pendleton man, John Greenwood, began the country's first short-distance horse-drawn omnibus service, and 110 years later, in 1934, Irlams O'Th'Height, on its north-western edge, became the starting point of Britain's first major trunk road, the East Lancashire Road.

Pendleton, 1902. St Thomas's Church (built 1831) and the former Pendleton Town Hall occupy the centre of the scene. To the left of the church is Ford Lane, leading, as its name implies, to the river crossing for Broughton. Behind the veranda (left) was the works of John Greenwood's omnibus undertaking, and later of the Manchester Carriage & Tramways Company. Starting as a toll collector at the Pendleton toll-gate, Greenwood (see also page 29) later became the licensee of the Horse Shoe Hotel, on the corner of Church Street (right), an ideal spot from which to supervise the traffic and the works. The width of the road at this point permitted a three-track layout for the electric tramways. The ornate poles supporting the wires found an additional use, but appeared rather top-heavy, when electric lights were added to their peaks to supplement the meagre street lighting of the pavement gas lamps. The street-centre poles were removed and replaced by side-mounted standards as motor traffic grew, but here the open-top tramcar has the road to itself, save for a lone cyclist. Church-goers in their Sunday best crowd the pavements. Now part of the busy A6 trunk road, the scene has vastly changed, and only the church remains. (W. Cox)

The plot of land which lay between the fork of the roads to Eccles (left) and Bolton (right) had been occupied by an inn since at least 1814. In 1903 a later building, the Woolpack Hotel, was offering Hardy's Celebrated Ales. Note the ornate lamp, which also housed a drinking fountain, and the horse-troughs, the latter a feature of most road junctions at that time. (W. Cox)

Eccles Old Road. July 1892, seen from the top deck of a horse-drawn tramcar. Until Eccles New Road opened, the old road was known as Sandy Lane. A pleasant, leafy lane, its large houses were protected by high walls, with lodges at the entrance gates. When a tramway was proposed in 1879, residents objected because of the increased noise and traffic it might bring.

Eccles Old Road, Chain Brow, alongside Hope Hall, *c.* 1904. A double-track electric tramway replaced the single-line horse tramway in 1903. It remains a recognisable spot on one of the most pleasant roads in the city, but the small boy would not venture into today's traffic as it heads for the nearby motorway junction. (H. Grundy)

Eccles Old Road, opposite Victoria Road, looking towards Eccles, 1930. The houses and cottages exist today, but in altered form. The gardens have been removed to give a wide pavement, and the cottages themselves converted into shops.

The second main road from Pendleton, Bolton Road, led to the boundary with Swinton at Irlams O'Th'Height. In this 1920s view, looking back to Pendleton, Bolton Road Methodist Church and Johnson's hardware shop are on the left. The row of small businesses beyond made it a popular shopping centre. Road improvement has ensured that nothing now remains. (Barrett)

Irlams O'Th'Height 'village', 1906. Formerly the site of another toll bar, here the road divided again, that to the right for Bolton, to the left for Swinton. In the fork of the road lay Westwood Methodist Chapel and the Britannia Inn. A wide road and an absence of traffic allows the lady's carriage to proceed unimpeded on the wrong side. (T.J.B. Whiteley)

Seedley from the air, 1927. In the south of Pendleton lie the districts of Seedley and Weaste, both having a high concentration of neat rows of terraced houses, typical of much of the city. In the centre of the picture is 'Chimney Pot Park', originally the two Highfield Reservoirs of the Salford Water Works, filled and converted for use as a public recreation ground. Properly titled Langworthy Park, it gained its better-known

unofficial name because of its great height. Players on its bowling greens and tennis courts found themselves level with the chimney pots of nearby houses. The road from left to right is Liverpool Street, where the school and church of St Ambrose face the high wall of the park. (NSR)

Thornfield Street, Weaste, *c.* 1905. Terraced houses constructed in the Victorian period were usually of the 'two-up two-down' type, lacking a bathroom, but with an outside toilet in the back yard. Supplies of pure water, together with proper sewage and drainage systems, helped in the general improvement in public health.

Bridson Street, Weaste, 1910. Houses boasting a lobby and/or a bay window were considered superior to the average two-up two-down type. In reality, they were not much different. In their time, both types offered better accommodation than had been available earlier. The off-licence (left) sold liquor to be consumed off the premises.

BROUGHTON

The district of Broughton lies to the north-east of the old Salford, separated from it by the River Irwell, and linked to it by only a few bridges. As a separate and largely rural district until 1853, it was, like Pendleton, a desirable residential area for the wealthier families. Greener, airier, and cleaner than its neighbour across the river, many of its houses were of the large detached villa type, occupied by city merchants and the like, who viewed Salfordians with distaste, and who were assimilated into the municipal borough very reluctantly. It was suspected that the riches of Broughton might be used to improve the lot of Salfordians.

The main roads through Broughton were, and remain, those connecting Manchester with Bury. The old road passed through the north-eastern edge of Broughton, and was turnpiked as early as 1754. A second route, Bury New Road, was newly created as a turnpike in 1831, and ran through the centre of the district, with a toll-gate at Kersal Bar. Before this date, country lanes had connected the hamlets around the ford and Broughton Spout. Industry and urbanisation came in the later part of the nineteenth century.

Broughton Suspension Bridge, 1883. Built in 1826 by landowner Fitzgerald to connect his Lower Broughton estates with the Pendleton side of the River Irwell, it was further downstream from the ford, and lasted until 1914. The Gerald Road footbridge was erected on the same site in 1924. (SLHL)

The Griffin Hotel, 1898. The original hostelry on Lower Broughton Road was alongside 'Ford View', so named because of its position overlooking the ford, which in 1882 became the site of Cromwell Bridge.

The replacement Griffin Hotel (left), seen here in 1911, was a much larger establishment in the same location on Lower Broughton Road. Cromwell Bridge is to the right. The electric tramcar waits ready to return on its route to Eccles via Manchester.

The inner end of Lower Broughton Road, seen in about 1924, was home to numerous small shops. The Meadow Dairy (right) was once a familiar name throughout the city. In the centre distance are the distinctive shapes of the Bee Hive and Poet's Corner public houses. (C. Wilkinson)

The junction of Lower Broughton Road, Frederick Road, and Camp Street, August 1939. Out of the picture (to the left) was St Boniface's School (see page 83), silent for the summer holidays, as the open-fronted tram makes its way over the points on a workman's special service to the docks. (WAC)

From Camp Street, Broughton Lane led through a pleasant residential area. Too narrow to accommodate a double track tramway, the line here was single with passing loops. The open-top tramcar is leaving the single line section as it approaches the junction with Great Clowes Street, c. 1911. (Grosvenor)

Great Clowes Street at its junction with Lower Broughton Road, viewed from Broughton Bridge, *c.* 1912. The Irwell Castle public house and the Victoria Theatre (whose foundation stone was laid by Sir Henry Irving in 1899) are to the right. (Grosvenor)

Broughton Public Baths on Great Clowes Street functioned from 1891 to 1935, a period when washing facilities for many local residents were limited to a stone sink and a portable tin bath, the latter usually dragged in from its storage nail in the back yard. First- and second-class swimming pools were incorporated. This photograph was probably taken around 1912. (Grosvenor)

The upper end of Great Clowes Street lay in the district of Higher Broughton, and had superior dwellings with small front gardens. In this winter picture, *c.* 1907, the tram tracks have been cleared of snow to enable services to continue.

Broughton Market Place, 1924. Bury New Road is the main thoroughfare through Higher Broughton, leading to the Prestwich boundary at Kersal Bar and on to Whitefield and Bury. The open-top tramcar makes its way towards Manchester. (JLB)

Great Cheetham Street East, seen at its junction with Bury New Road in the mid-1920s, was the shopping centre for Higher Broughton. The increasing number of road vehicles, not evident in this picture, required a police constable to control the junction. (JLB)

Bury New Road, Kersal, 1903. The Higher Broughton tramway terminus, this was formerly the site of the toll-bar, the gate-keeper's house (left) surviving to this day, though it is now sadly neglected. The cabmen's shelter stands in the entrance to Moor Lane. (Miller)

Kersal Moor and St Paul's Church, 1903. Kersal Moor was the home of the Manchester Races from the late 1600s until 1847, when a new course was opened at Castle Irwell. Note the hay-making (centre foreground). (Miller)

Kersal Cell, located by the river off Littleton Road, is, in parts, the oldest building in the city. Owned for many years by the family of John Byrom (1692–1763), poet and hymn-writer, it survives because of several preservation attempts.

HORSE-DRAWN
PASSENGER TRANSPORT

In the nineteenth century horse-drawn vehicles enjoyed a monopoly on the roads. The canals and the railways had captured much of the long-distance traffic, but local journeys for both goods and passengers depended upon the horse. The Turnpike Trusts had improved the surfaces of the main roads, and John Greenwood, a toll-gate keeper at Pendleton, aware of the steadily increasing flow of people between the suburbs and the town centre, established the first omnibus service between Pendleton and Manchester in 1824. The success of his venture attracted competitors into the business, and by 1850 all the main roads in the area had regular omnibus services. Competition grew so fierce that in 1865 the various proprietors merged their interests to form the Manchester Carriage Company, offering a unified passenger transport system throughout the area.

The cobbled surfaces of the roads, though an improvement on earlier conditions, still ensured a fairly rough ride. A smoother ride was offered in 1861 by John Greenwood, Jun., who constructed an early form of guide-wheel tramway on part of his father's original route. The invention of the grooved rail superseded his efforts, and the 1870 Tramways Act encouraged the Salford Council to construct a tramway system of its own, which was leased by the Carriage Company from 1877 to 1901.

The Victoria Arch entrance to Peel Park forms the backdrop for this 1866 picture of a Manchester Carriage Company omnibus as it halts on the way to Manchester. In the roadway may be noted the rails of Greenwood's 1861 guide-wheel tramway. (SLHL)

For the commencement of services on the 1877 tramway, 30 double-ended tramcars were ordered from the Starbuck Company of Birkenhead. Later relegated to part-day use, one is seen here on the Eccles New Road route to Weaste.

John Eades was a former Greenwood coachbuilder who rose to become Manager of the Carriage Company's Works at Pendleton. In 1877 he patented a reversible tramcar, whose body could be rotated on its truck when the car reached a terminus, thus obviating the need to unhitch the horses. Eades reversible cars, needing only one staircase, were shorter, lighter, cheaper to construct, occupied less depot space, and needed fewer horses, so it was not surprising that his design was adopted and built under licence in many towns of the British Isles. In the Pendleton Works alone, over 500 were built for the Company between 1877 and 1900. In 1898 Eades adapted a horse-tram to run on electric power drawn from storage batteries, but allowed this modern concept to lapse, possibly because of the fragmentation of the Company's monopoly. On Regent Road in 1894, the Eades tramcar was adorned with flags celebrating Queen Victoria's visit to open the Ship Canal. The buildings behind the tram include a second-hand furniture shop and one bearing on its wall the old sign for an undertaker – a coffin lid!

Two Eades reversible cars pass on Bury New Road in the 1890s. The track in the foreground led into Knoll Street and the side entrance of the Higher Broughton Depot. It was cheaper to ride on the open top than inside the lower saloon. Note the lady with bassinette.

The staff of the Manchester Carriage & Tramways Company's Pendleton office, Broad Street, 1890. The white-bearded figure is Robert Guest, first employed by Greenwood in 1848, who became local area manager for the Company, and retired in 1901 after 53 years' service.

Trafford Road, Salford, in the 1890s, at the termination of a race meeting on the New Barns course. Thousands of race-goers were transported to and from the main Manchester railway stations at a fare of sixpence. All available vehicles were pressed into service. (SLHL)

Several horse-drawn omnibus proprietors competed with the Company in private-hire work. Frederick J. Knott, of Weaste, supplied this vehicle for an all-male outing from a local hostelry near Derwent Street in about 1900. (Mrs B. Knott)

Day trippers (again male only) pose for the camera before leaving in a Henry Grieve wagonette, pre-First World War. The wagonette was the preferred choice for longer journeys, though the hard seats would not offer a particularly comfortable ride. Canvas awnings provided limited protection in wet weather.

Bury New Road/Knoll Street, 1975. The Manchester Carriage Company's Higher Broughton depot complex, comprising courtyard, stables, lamp and harness rooms, forge, yard-master's house, and so on, survived relatively intact until the 1980s, when, despite its listed status, it was lost through neglect and Council indifference. (E. Gray)

THE RIVER IRWELL

The River Irwell rises in the hills of North Lancashire and flows mainly southwards through some of the old cotton towns before reaching Salford at Agecroft, where its banks have been home to a rowing club since the 1860s and have seen many splendid regattas. The river's meandering course takes it thence around Castle Irwell, which until 1963 was the site of the Manchester Racecourse, now occupied by Salford University halls of residence.

Onwards through Lower Broughton to the Crescent and the Adelphi, the river begins to form the boundary between Salford and Manchester near Strangeways. Victoria Bridge, by Manchester Cathedral, was regarded as the limit of navigation for boats on the Mersey & Irwell system. Downstream from Victoria Bridge, the river flows past the sites of the old eighteenth-century quays and warehouses, before reaching Regent Bridge, from where in 1894 its course to the sea was appropriated by the Manchester Ship Canal. Thus, the twentieth-century Irwell provides the water for the canal, but apparently vanishes at the point where the docklands begin. Heavily polluted by industry in the eighteenth and nineteenth centuries, the river is now much cleaner and fish stocks are recovering.

Away from the industrial areas, the Irwell's course through Salford had its green and attractive lengths, as this 1920s view shows. From the upper end of Lower Broughton Road, a district known as 'The Cliff', the leafy heights of Kersal may be viewed (right), while below (left) were the stables of the Racecourse. (JLB)

At 'The Cliff' the river undercuts the high ground, with an ever-present danger of land-slips, of which there have been several over the years. This section of Great Clowes Street collapsed in 1927. The houses here are still occupied today, but lack a road frontage. (SLHL)

A 1930 aerial view of the river by the Adelphi and Silk Street, looking downstream towards Broughton Bridge and Great Clowes Street (top right). Lower Broughton (top left) and Blackfriars (right) show the concentration of terraced houses. Factories are interspersed, mainly closer to the river's edge, for many took water from the river for use in industrial processes, and, furthermore, found it a convenient channel into which to discharge waste products. Adelphi Street became home to Salford Electrical Industries. In 1930 the large white building (centre right) was occupied by Boots the Chemists. Before the Clean Air Act, pictures such as this tended to be taken on summer Sundays, when the atmosphere was more likely to be free of smoke from household fires and factory chimneys. (NSR)

Lower Kersal, November 1980. Despite various preventative measures, parts of Lower Broughton have always been subject to flooding when the water level in the Irwell is raised after heavy rains in the Pennines. (SLHL)

Victoria Bridge, upstream from Blackfriars Bridge, 1859. This was an 1839 structure on the site of the Old Salford Bridge, the traditional crossing point between Salford and Manchester. Factories and small boats line the banks. The tower of Manchester Cathedral is in course of reconstruction. (SLHL)

Albert Bridge, 1896. Small steamers plying from the New Bailey Street landing stage carried sightseers to the new Ship Canal docks. Earlier, they had offered a passenger service as far as Warrington and Runcorn on the former Mersey & Irwell Navigation system. Both banks of the river along this length between Regent Bridge and Victoria Bridge were lined with the warehouses of the old river navigation, and, although the new terminal docks were downstream, cargoes were often transshipped into small barges, which continued to bring goods to the old quays. New Bailey Street was named after the nearby New Bailey prison, and its bridge was erected in 1844. Beyond the bridge, the Salford bank (left) was the site of the original Salford Quay, where, at the time of writing, Quay Street (not to be confused with the Quay Street on the Manchester side) survives in an area the city planners have chosen to call Chapel Wharf in an attempt to avoid confusion with the newer Salford Quays development in the old docklands. The landing stage is now the site of the Mark Addy public house, named in honour of a local hero who, in Victorian times, rescued many people from drowning. (MSCCo)

Mode Wheel Mill, Lock, and Weir, 1889. Since 1894 the River Irwell has discharged its water into the terminal docks of the Ship Canal. In earlier times, owners of mills constructed weirs to give a good head of water to power the water-wheel, but the weirs impeded navigation. Old weirs may still be seen on the Irwell at Pendleton (from Littleton Road Bridge) and at the Adelphi (from the Crescent), but that at Mode Wheel was destroyed, along with the mill, in the construction of the Ship Canal. Boatmen on the old river navigation negotiated the difference in levels via a lock, which cut through the weir alongside the mill. At Mode Wheel (Maud's Wheel on early maps) the water-mill ground corn and crushed logwood for dyes. Behind the mill, by the wall of Weaste Cemetery, was a mooring basin, where river flats loaded and discharged their cargoes. The Mode Wheel Locks of the Ship Canal were constructed slightly to the south of the original site, and are the furthest inland of the five sets of locks which raise and lower vessels some 60 feet between Salford and the sea. (MSCCo)

Trafford Road and Bridge, 1889. The original Trafford Bridge spanned the Irwell to connect with Stretford at the end of what was almost a country lane. The view looks from Salford towards the trees of Trafford Park.

Trafford Road Swing Bridge, 1894. In the construction of the Ship Canal, a new excavation was made to allow ships to take a less severe bend. Viewed from the opposite direction, the original bridge (in the previous picture) is seen beyond the new Swing Bridge. (MSCCo)

Salford Docks, 1935. After a hesitant start in 1894, traffic on the Manchester Ship Canal grew steadily. The import of raw cotton for the textile trade, and the export of finished goods, had been the mainspring for the construction of the canal. In addition, grain, timber, and oil featured prominently among the imports, and Salford Docks became the outlet for a wide variety of manufactured goods from the region's factories. In this 1935 view, Number 8 Dock held one of Manchester Liners' own vessels, the *Manchester Exporter* (centre), which was engaged in the Canadian trade. The *Pandion* (left) and *Serula* (right), both vessels of the British & Continental Steamship Company, offered regular services carrying mixed cargoes to and from Holland, Belgium, and northern France. (Stewart Bale)

In 1901 the Company purchased the Manchester Racecourse, which, since 1867, had been located on land by the river at New Barns, between Trafford Road and Mode Wheel. The Manchester Races then moved back to their previous home at Castle Irwell, and the Canal Company gained space on which to construct extensive railway sidings and an additional large dock. By 1904 the traffic on the Ship Canal was exceeded in value only by that of London, Liverpool, Hull, and Glasgow. The new dock, Number 9, over half a mile in length, and equipped with the latest handling equipment, was officially opened by King Edward VII in 1905. Here, floating pneumatic grain elevators (left) suck grain from the holds, and discharge into barges alongside for onward transmission elsewhere. (Stewart Bale)

Number 9 Dock, 1922. A grain storage elevator, built in 1915 and having a capacity of 40,000 tons, stood at the head of Number 9 Dock, connected to the discharging berths by conveyor belts running in subways beneath the wharves. (Sankey)

The main headquarters of the Canal Company were in Manchester, but the local administrative offices gained a new building on Trafford Road in 1927, where the entrance arch, though in Salford, bore the title 'Manchester Docks'. (Downs)

An expanse of water, enabling large ships to be swung round for their return journey to the sea, lay opposite the end of Number 8 Dock. A dredger (right) is engaged on the never-ending task of removing silt from the Canal bed, in 1922. (Sankey)

Mode Wheel Locks, 1935. The locks raised or lowered ships 15 feet, while the sluices maintained a constant level in the terminal docks. To conserve supplies of water, the locks were constructed in pairs, only the largest vessels using the large dock. (A.H. Clarke)

In terms of tonnage handled, the peak years of the Ship Canal were in the 1950s. During the war period, and afterwards as exports revived, dockers often worked through the night to achieve a rapid turn-round of ships, for ship-owners regarded time spent in port as idle. The floating crane is silhouetted against the night sky as the Furness Withy vessel *Pacific Exporter* loads Morris cars for export to North America in 1948. Whereas ships of the Manchester Liners traded to east coast ports of Canada and the United States, the Furness Withy 'Pacific' vessels maintained regular sailings via the Panama Canal to west coast ports of North America until 1970. Thereafter, the number of ships using the Canal grew less, as manufacturing industry declined. Manchester Liners ceased to operate their Canadian services from Manchester in 1979. Patterns of trade had altered, losses mounted, and in the early 1980s the Company considered complete closure of the upper reaches of the Canal. Since then, the prestigious Salford Quays development, a mixture of high-quality residential, business, hotel, and leisure interests, has transformed and revitalised the former docklands. (MSCCo)

RAILWAYS

The original plan for the 1830 Liverpool & Manchester Railway located its terminus in Salford on land by New Bailey Street, but a subsequent change took the line across the river to Liverpool Road, Manchester. The Salford length was described as 'passing at no great distance from several country seats, whose rich lawns and flourishing plantations afford an agreeable variety' – evidently a reference to the large houses in Weaste and Pendleton, which could be seen from the train. This length later gained stations at Weaste (1838–1942), Seedley (1882–1956), Cross Lane (1831–1959), and Ordsall Lane (1849–1957).

The Manchester & Bolton Railway opened in 1838, with its terminus in Salford on a viaduct by New Bailey Street. A halt at Windsor Bridge moved to Pendleton (1843–1966). In 1844 the Liverpool & Manchester line was extended into Salford Station and onwards to meet lines from Yorkshire in Victoria Station. By 1887 the Lancashire & Yorkshire Railway had constructed a new line to Liverpool via a second Pendleton 'New' (Broad Street) Station.

Manchester Exchange Station, 1884. A favourite question posed by radio quizmasters of old was 'What do Manchester Racecourse, Manchester Docks, and Manchester Exchange Station have in common?' The answer was that they were not in Manchester – they were all in Salford. Exchange Station was opened by the London & North Western Railway in 1884 to relieve congestion in Victoria. Viewed from Lower Chapel Street, the station frontage surmounts the approach roads, with the gloomy access to Greengate (left) passing beneath the tracks. (NRM)

A Lancashire & Yorkshire Railway train leaving Manchester (Victoria) passes the LNWR's Exchange Station as it crosses into Salford, pre-1923. The headboard 'B' indicated Blackpool Central as the destination. Many businessmen travelled daily from the Fylde coast on so-called 'club' trains.

Two trains pass on the wide viaducts linking Salford with Exchange Station, date not known. The number of tracks had been augmented by LNWR and L&Y extensions and were dominated by signal gantries. Threlfall's brewery rises above the parapet.

New Bailey Street Goods Yard, 1930. The land between Salford Station (centre left) and the river, occupied by the New Bailey prison until 1871, was acquired by the L&Y Railway Company for an extension to the existing goods yard, from which it was separated by Irwell Street. The lines from Bolton and the connection to the Liverpool &

Manchester line (bottom right) were built on viaducts, so the goods yard, being at a lower level, was reached by steeply graded ramps. Locomotives crossing Irwell Street were limited to not more than ten wagons at any one time, and were preceded by a flagman until the end in 1964. (NSR)

The ornate pillars of the colonnade supporting the main line could be viewed from ground level in the New Bailey Street Goods Yard. Additional tracks had added two further bridges (in different styles) to the original at Salford Station by the 1920s, when this photograph was taken. (F. Foxall)

The L&Y had further extensive sidings in Pendleton at Brindle Heath Junction, where in 1910 the signalman was startled by tank engine 494 reversing into his cabin. (SLHL)

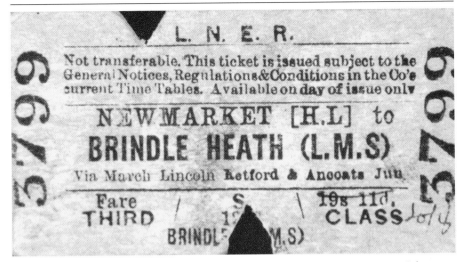

NEWMARKET [H.L] to
BRINDLE HEATH (L.M.S)
Via March Lincoln Retford & Ancoats Jun.

Fare / S. \ 19s 11d.
THIRD / 1 \ CLASS

BRINDL (M.S)

A 1931 ticket to Brindle Heath, where there was no passenger station, might seem puzzling. However, it may be assumed that it was for a stable-boy accompanying a horse from Newmarket to the nearby Castle Irwell Racecourse. (Godfrey Croughton)

In 1888 the L&Y established an engine shed at Agecroft, close to the Brindle Heath Junction, where the lines to Bolton and Wigan diverged. Concerned mainly with freight trains, particularly from local collieries, it closed in 1966. It is seen here before 1923. (RP)

The L&Y opened a small island-platform station at Irlams O'Th'Height in 1901. Here, in 1917, the L&Y appointed its first Station Mistress, and it became staffed entirely by ladies. An excursion train approaches from the Manchester direction. (RP)

Irlams O'Th'Height Station, 1912. Situated on the embankment, high above Bank Lane, the station was too far removed from the main road to compete with the tramways for local traffic to Manchester. It closed in 1956.

The Manchester Ship Canal Company operated a large private railway system on the docks, with connections to the LNWR at Weaste and the L&Y at Windsor Bridge. Until 1916 its locomotives were named after ports of the world. *Kurrachee* was a Hudswell Clarke engine of 1903. (MSCCo)

The age of steam was nearly at an end in 1966 when Ship Canal locomotive 58 was photographed at Mode Wheel. Diesel locomotives had begun to take over in 1959, and most steam engines had been withdrawn by 1967. (E. Gray)

Tickets issued at local stations. In 1923 railways were grouped into the 'Big Four', and Salford lines became part of the London, Midland & Scottish Railway. In 1948 the LMSR was absorbed into the nationalised system.

1. LNWR Manchester Exchange to Patricroft, Third Class, 4d.
2. L&Y Pendleton, reduced fare for serviceman on leave.
3. LMSR Salford to Victoria, Third Class, 1d.
4. LMSR Ordsall Lane to Cross Lane, Third Class.
5. LMSR Pendleton (Broad Street) to Salford, Third Class Single.
6. LMSR Seedley to Blackpool, Evening Excursion.
7. British Railways Cross Lane to Morecambe Half-Day Excursion.
8. British Railways Irlams O'Th'Height to Pendlebury, Third Class Single, 2d.

During the construction of the Ship Canal (1887–1894), many of the contractor's locomotives were named after places close to the Canal. *Salford* was a Manning Wardle engine of 1888. The names *Broughton, Pendleton, Seedley, Weaste,* and *Irwell* were used also.

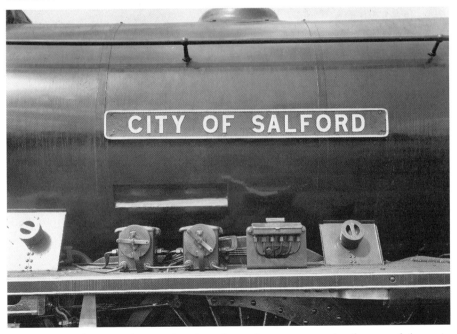

The practice of naming locomotives has always been an attractive feature of the main line railways. Salford was honoured in 1948, when the name *City of Salford* was applied to an LMS-designed Stanier 'Pacific' loco. (British Railways)

Ex-LMSR locomotives continued in service for the nationalised railways, but with the prefix '4' added to their numbers. 'Patriot' class 45503 *Royal Leicestershire Regiment* crosses Chapel Street in 1959 as it passes Deal Street signal box on the run into Manchester. (J.R. Carter)

Ex-LMSR 'Jubilee' 45700 *Amethyst* pulls out of Exchange Station with a Glasgow express in 1962. The buildings of Exchange, badly damaged in a 1940 air raid, were never fully repaired, but the station continued in use until 1969. (J.R. Carter)

Section Seven

ELECTRIC TRAMWAYS

On the expiration of the Manchester Carriage Company's lease of the Salford horse tramways in 1901, the Corporation purchased a number of the Company's tramcars and horses in order to continue services during the transitional period. The first electric route, along Bury New Road to Kersal Bar, opened in October 1901. Other routes were speedily converted, and lines were extended into adjoining districts, for Salford had agreed to provide the services in Eccles, Swinton, Prestwich, and Whitefield.

The last horse-tram ran in 1903, and the new system, with its vehicles in a splendid livery of chocolate and cream, with lining-out in gold, was virtually complete by 1906. Additions thereafter were of a minor nature, but more new tramcars were purchased, and existing ones were improved by the fitting of covered tops and platform vestibules. A programme of rebuilding the open cars was continued in the 1920s, when the last new tramcars brought the fleet total to 230. Joint cross-Manchester routes were instituted in 1926, but competition from the more flexible motor bus hindered further development. In the 1930s the number of tramway routes declined as motor bus services increased. The tramways would have been abandoned by 1940 but for the onset of the Second World War, and its consequent shortage of imported fuel. As it was, the few remaining tram services soldiered on, confined within the old city boundary, until new replacement motor buses became available in 1947.

Bury New Road, 1903. The horse-trams had no fixed stops, but the electric cars halted only at designated stopping places. An important boarding point was Kersal, on the Whitefield route, where two open-top cars await passengers.

An early open-top tramcar in Cross Lane passes the Regent (later the Palace) Theatre and the Ship Hotel as it approaches the junction, c. 1903. Until 1912 an ornate centre pole supported the overhead wires. (See also page 63.)

For Salford tramcars to carry workers into Trafford Park, track and overhead wires had to align accurately when the Trafford Road Bridge swung back into position, a problem solved by the Ship Canal Engineer in 1905. (JLB)

Trafford Road remained an important tramway route right to the end in 1947. Car 373, seen leaving Trafford Bridge in 1938, was originally a 1903 open-top vehicle, which retained its open ends even when fitted with a top-cover. (WAC)

Frederick Road Depot opened in 1901 to house the new electric tramcar fleet. Extensions, including the red-brick arch and offices of 1907, were added as the fleet grew to its maximum total of 230 vehicles. In the 1920s congestion caused by the need to garage motor buses alongside the trams led to the construction of a second depot, which opened in 1929 at Weaste. Though intended mainly for buses, Weaste Depot incorporated a number of tram tracks also. Emerging from the Frederick Road Depot archway in this 1930 picture is tramcar 112, originally an open-top car, rebuilt in 1920 to all-enclosed style. A 'Redline' lorry delivers barrels of fuel. There is a preservation order on the arch, but the sheds and workshops beyond, after serving as a bus garage until 1986, have been demolished. (Stansfeld Parker)

The Cross Lane/Trafford Road/Regent Road/Eccles New Road tramway junction was of the 'Grand Union' type, with two lines each way across and round every corner, together with nearby crossovers, and a network of overhead wires. The 'Collins Automatic Point Changer', the invention of a Salford man, ensured that the points could be set from the tramcar by the motorman keeping his power on, or off, according to his desired direction, as he approached the junction. In wet weather, such as this day in 1939, the sudden movement of a point blade would send up a little spout of water, fascinating to the ever-present onlookers leaning on the pavement guard rails at this spot. One of the busiest tramway junctions in the country, it was subject to great wear, and consequently was renewed and relaid in 1912, and again in 1935. After the abandonment of the tramways in 1947, the track became buried under successive layers of tarmac. During the construction of the M602 motorway, the contractors uncovered and salvaged the junction, albeit in pieces, for possible reconstruction at the National Tramway Museum in Derbyshire. (WAC)

By the outbreak of war in 1939 only five tram routes remained. At Irlams O'Th'Height, abandonment of the Swinton and Pendlebury services had enabled the shortened tram route to terminate at a pedestrian refuge in the middle of Bolton Road. (*Daily Herald*)

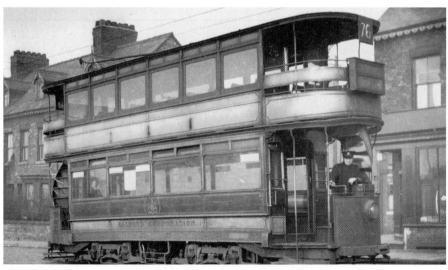

The last open-fronted tram to remain in service was photographed in Eccles New Road on 1 March 1947, the last day of operation to Weaste. Its run-down condition was typical of much of the fleet at that time. The remaining routes finished on 31 March. (R.B. Parr)

HORSE POWER

Towards the end of the Victorian era, new methods of propulsion were under consideration. Steam power had been known on the railways and in the factories for a considerable time, and steam-driven tramcars ran from Bury to Higher Broughton in 1883. In Trafford Park, tramcars powered by gas engines ran from 1896 until 1908, and on the main roads of the city electric tramcars successfully replaced horse-drawn tramcars in 1901–3.

The advent of the electric tram in 1901 was only shortly in advance of the city's first motor vehicles, which were licensed in 1904. Yet, despite the successful application of mechanical traction, horse-drawn vehicles survived for a surprisingly long period of time. It was not unusual to see milk roundsmen, ice-cream vendors, or rag-and-bone scrap merchants, making deliveries or selling from horse-drawn carts until well into the second half of the twentieth century.

H.J. Gaskell's cart, Seedley, 1905. Horse-drawn open milk-floats made daily door-to-door deliveries of fresh milk. A steel measure, filled by dipping it into a large churn, was used to pour the required amount into the customer's jug.

Anslow's bread van, Holland Street, 1905. Anslow's enjoyed a high reputation in Salford for quality bakery products, even in the difficult rationing period of the Second World War, and survived into the 1950s. (SLHL)

Horse-power of a different kind was paraded at the Town Hall in Bexley Square in 1904, when these early supporters of the petrol engine lined up their vehicles for inspection. On the extreme right is a De Dion 8 hp car with registration BA 1.

BA 1 was the first of 32 motor cars registered in Salford in 1904. BA 139, a 12 hp Singer car, pictured here outside its lean-to garage in Weaste, was registered in May 1907. (G. Greenhalgh)

Seaford Road, 1907. Horsfall & Bickham, of Pendleton, manufactured Horbick motor vehicles up to 1920. The Tramways Department supported the local firm by purchasing a 12 hp van (BA 288, £325) and an open lorry (BA 289, £370).

Frederick Road Depot Yard, 1912. Another motor vehicle used by the Tramways Department was this Halley 34 hp chain-drive lorry, fitted with a tower for overhead line work.

Motor vehicles became much more common after the First World War. J. & T. Rothwell, wholesale grocers, acquired several delivery vans. BA 2449 was a 30 hp solid-tyred Burford lorry, new in 1919–20, and number 12 in the fleet. (SLHL)

Taxi-cabs did good business during race meetings at Castle Irwell, as this photograph (dating from before 1914) shows. Cabs wait outside Tattersall's Stand to take the punters back to main line railway stations at the end of the day.

Stott Lane, 1926. Steam-power survived on the roads throughout the first half of the century. Topham Brothers, of Weaste, had a fleet of Sentinel steam wagons, notable for the glow of the fire beneath the driver's cab and the ash dropped on the road. (SLHL)

Steam survived, too, in the shape of the heavy and slow road rollers, once commonly used by the Highways Department to smooth road surfaces. In a 1923 collision with a tramcar on Bury New Road, this roller suffered most.

A long-established furniture removal and haulage firm was that of Samuel R. Teggin, who also offered charabancs for hire and established the Salford Motor Mart. His premises were at the corner of Langworthy Road, centre left in this 1928 view of Eccles New Road. (C. Wilkinson)

Teggin's firm survived to the Second World War and beyond. A new ERF lorry betrays its wartime origin under blackout regulations (1939–45) by having headlamp masks and luminous paint on the fenders.

The car used by the Mayor of Salford has traditionally carried the registration RJ 1, the RJ allocation following the earlier BA sequences from 1931. In earlier years, the mayoral carriage had a variety of forms, and a variety of registrations. In 1912 the Mayor was allowed the use of a Crossley landaulette, BA 822, bought by the Tramways as a relief cash van, provided he notified the Department of his requirements on Mondays. Other cars for his exclusive use came later, but were always cared for by the Tramways Department. In 1958 this Daimler limousine, seen outside the entrance to the Peel Park Library and Art Gallery, replaced a Rolls-Royce. (EMC)

Horse-power of the genuine sort was still to be seen in the city, albeit with the modern accessory of pneumatic tyres. This scrap merchant's cart was photographed near Orange Street, Pendleton, in 1978. (SLHL)

MARKETS & SHOPS

A weekly market and an annual fair had been held in Salford since 1228. The traditional site was likely to have been on Chapel Street, near the end of Greengate, where the original township grew up close to Salford Bridge, the main crossing point of the Irwell. Shopkeepers and tradesmen catering for the needs of the rising population became established as the town grew, and in Victorian times, the streets of terraced houses almost always had their general store, or corner shop close at hand. Cross Lane, Broad Street, Bolton Road, and Regent Road developed as busy, prosperous shopping streets.

At 88 Regent Road, William Timpson established the first of his chain of shoeshops, and on the same road in 1931 Salford gained its first Woolworth's store. In 1939 a new market centre opened on the site of the former cattle market in Cross Lane. Alongside was the venue for the visiting fairgrounds at holiday times. Today, shopping is largely concentrated in supermarkets and malls, reached by taxi or private car. The once-lively streets have been destroyed by road 'improvements', most of the corner shops have gone, and lost, too, is the friendly specialist advice once so readily available.

Trinity Market, Chapel Street, 1901, better known as 'Flat Iron Market' because of its triangular shape. Many stalls specialised in the sale of second-hand clothing. The arched roof of Exchange Station (left) hovers over the scene. Centre right is the old Police Station, surviving today as a stationer's shop.

The confined limits of 'Flat Iron Market' may be seen in this view from the corner of Blackfriars Street on a wet day in 1920. Having existed on this site for centuries, the market closed in 1939 on the opening of the new Cross Lane Market. (SLHL)

The Cross Lane Cattle Market, c. 1905. It was founded in 1774 and occupied an extensive site, with its own bank, and an abattoir nearby. Animals arrived by rail at cattle sidings, from where they were herded to market, and displayed for sale in large pens.

Cross Lane, 1948. At the entrance to the new 1939 market stood a modernistic clock tower (centre left). The old Cattle Market Hotel (left) faced across the road to the Cattle Market Tavern and the Craven Heifer Hotel. (Valentine)

Ellor Street, 1960. Off Cross Lane, and running roughly parallel to Broad Street, this was another busy shopping street, penetrating the area known colloquially as 'Hanky Park' (Hankinson Street). It was destroyed to make room for high-rise flats.

One of the shops on Ellor Street was that of Thomas Parker, butcher, seen displaying his wares in 1906. Note the carcasses hanging outside, a practice which today would be condemned as unhygienic.

William Pannifer's Poultry Shop, in tiny premises by the corner of Western Street and Seedley Park Road, displayed a range of birds for Christmas 1908.

Wetherall & Company, with the motto 'Honour Bright', had a chain of grocery shops throughout the area. One of the first to claim that they were never knowingly undersold, the Company advertised 'Quality The Highest, Prices The Lowest'. This photograph dates from before 1912.

In the poorer areas of Salford, pawnbrokers thrived, and there was a steady trade in second-hand goods. Thomas Williams' store, established 1877 in Lower Broughton, dealt in furniture and clothing. Note the clothes wringer, or mangle, outside the shop (bottom right).

The Pendleton Co-operative & Industrial Society once had such extensive and varied business interests (including a funeral service), that it could claim to provide for its customers' every need from birth until death. This is Grocery Branch No. 18, 1910.

J.H. Hargreaves, in Great Cheetham Street, Broughton, 1913, was a newsagent and stationer, whose premises also housed the branch post office.

A typical corner shop in an area of dense terraced housing was this off-licence and general grocery store in Derby Street, Ordsall, managed by Charles Thornton in 1909. The Groves & Whitnall brewery was close by at Regent Bridge.

Oldfield Road, once a farmland area, was built up and industrialised in Victorian times. Rows of small shops lined the pavements. Samuel Livesey ran his grocery store at number 22 for 55 years until his death in 1938.

Cycling was at first a popular pastime, but then became important as a cheap means of transport to and from work. The Weaste Tyre Repair Company offered spares and services to the bicycle owners around Eccles New Road in the 1920s.

Section Ten

EDUCATION & HEALTH

The first National School in Salford dated from 1813, at which time formal education was available to only a limited number of children, often through the efforts of religious movements or voluntary groups. Just as today's universities are sponsored by business interests, in Victorian times the demands of local industry for skilled labour influenced the curriculum of schools, and led to the development of higher education via Mechanics Institutes in Salford (1838) and Pendleton (1850), and the Salford Working Men's College (1873). The Education Act of 1879 established a national system of elementary schools for 5 to 13 year olds, and the Salford School Board also set up Higher Grade schools for selected pupils who desired continuing education. The twentieth century has seen successive raisings of the school-leaving age, the reorganisation of secondary education, and the establishment of Salford University.

Public health steadily improved from the Victorian period, when Medical Officers worked to eradicate prevalent diseases, and campaigned against the pollution of the air and the river. The first smokeless zones were instituted in 1955, and such astonishing progress was made that in 1973 the city gained a Clean Air Award.

The Salford Royal Technical Institute in Peel Park opened in 1896. It was one of the first such municipal colleges in the country, offering specialist instruction for local industrial requirements. (Grosvenor)

The Technical College became part of the new University in 1967. The University's costly and short-lived Peel Tower, an eyesore demolished in 1994, was sited inappropriately between the College and the Art Gallery – a planning scandal! (E. Gray)

Present-day physical education evolved from exercises known as 'drill'. Fully clothed children in the playground of St Boniface's School, Frederick Road, exercise with weights in 1905.

During the First World War, some Salford schools were taken over as military hospitals for the less seriously wounded. Nurses and medical orderlies pose for the camera in the playground of Langworthy Road School, 1916.

Salford Grammar School for boys began in 1904 as a day-school housed in the Technical College. Its new 1914 Leaf Square building was requisitioned as a hospital, the boys returning after the war. A 1934 group shows Headmaster Mr J.G. Altham (left) and Mr Hindshaw (right).

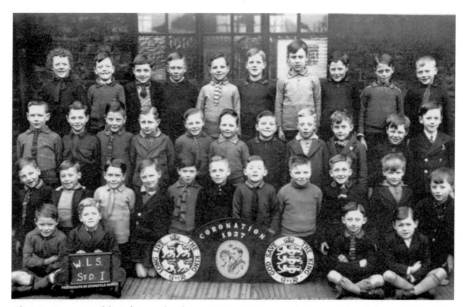

The seven-year-olds of Standard 1 at West Liverpool Street Elementary School in Coronation Year, 1937. The author is on the extreme right of the front row. (Stansfeld Parker)

Broomhouse Lane School on Eccles Old Road, *c.* 1908. The school gained its name from the former title of that length of road. It closed in 1972.

Hope Hospital evolved from its beginnings as the Salford Union Infirmary, or Workhouse, in 1882. The fields seen in this 1909 view are now covered with modern extensions to this fine teaching hospital.

Salford Royal Hospital, closed in the early 1990s, had its origin in 1827, when a medical charity established a small dispensary. The hospital constructed on the same site was subsequently extended. The patch of new brickwork in this 1912 view shows a former entrance.

Ladywell Hospital on Eccles New Road opened in 1892 as an isolation unit for patients suffering from infectious diseases. It gained its name from a nearby well, whose pure water was claimed to have healing properties.

EMERGENCY – FIRE, POLICE, AMBULANCE

In 1844 the Salford police force consisted of a Chief Constable, 4 inspectors and 37 policemen; by 1898 this total had risen to 330. In 1868 the Borough Fire Brigade had become the responsibility of the police. This section was staffed by 15 'Fire Policemen', who had two manual fire-engines for use in Salford, one for Pendleton, and one for Broughton.

The first steam-powered pump (horse-drawn) was acquired in 1875. Another followed, and seven local police stations were provided with carts carrying fire hoses. Superintendent Bentley was appointed as the first Chief Fire Officer in 1898. The new Fire Station on The Crescent was designed to house horse-drawn appliances, the first motor-driven engines arriving in 1910. In the same year 36 'Gamewell' Fire Alarm boxes were installed at various locations in the town.

The Salford Police Force amalgamated with Manchester's in 1968 and the Fire Brigade joined the Greater Manchester Fire Service in 1974.

The old Fire Station at Ford Street, near the Town Hall, took delivery in 1894 of a horse-drawn fire escape with extending ladder, supplied from John Shaw's Wellington Street Works. It could be united with its front portion to form a four-wheeled vehicle. Through the windows (left) may be glimpsed one of the steam pumps.

While the steam pumps and escapes were hauled by horse-power, the carts on which the hoses and smaller equipment were carried in the 1890s relied on man-power. The use of pedal-cycles to tow the carts was not a success. (SLHL)

The Crescent Fire Station (1903) is now the Viewpoint Gallery. It was designed so that appliances could enter from the rear, and thus be facing the front exit ready for any emergency. Ambulances were garaged to the right. (JLB)

A solid-tyred fire engine with turntable escape ladder at the Central (Crescent) Fire Station in the 1920s. The small garages beyond housed ambulances and prison vans ('black marias'). Pendleton and Broughton had sub-stations, with their own allocation of appliances. (SLHL)

The traditional shape of fire engines changed during and after the Second World War. A Dennis appliance of 1969, retaining the familiar red colour, but showing off the new profile, stands in line for the weekly Friday morning wash. (D. Heywood)

Three 10 hp Ford cars were purchased by the police in 1937 to replace some motor cycle and sidecar combinations. RJ 8201 passes along The Crescent, opposite the Central Fire Station and Cenotaph. Off the picture to the left was the site selected for the new police headquarters. Across the road, a red-and-cream Salford bus heads for Swinton on the old route 19. (*Daily Herald*)

In 1927 the Salford Force introduced a Police Box system. Forty-one stout wooden huts, or boxes, fitted with telephones and first aid equipment for emergencies, were erected at strategic sites around the city at a cost of £17 each. Before the days of mobile radios, the boxes proved valuable in allowing foot patrols to keep in contact with headquarters. They were also strong enough to hold an offender until assistance arrived. The boxes remained in use until the 1950s. Pictured is the one at the corner of Victoria Road and Eccles Old Road.

The Ship Canal Company established its own Dock Police Force and Fire Brigade in 1893. At first all constables had to have fire-fighting training. A fireboat, the *Firefly*, capable of throwing 4,000 gallons of water per minute, was maintained in Salford Docks, and the assistance of the Salford brigade could be called upon if required. The police constables wore a uniform similar to that of local forces, except for the badge on the helmet. At peak strength, over 100 constables were employed to enforce the law and supervise security on dock land. The force was disbanded in 1993.

Major C.V. Godfrey, Chief Constable 1908–46, was responsible for many innovations, particularly concerning road safety – play streets (areas closed to traffic) in 1930, first automatic traffic lights in 1932. He is seen with King George VI in a 1941 wartime inspection. (SLHL)

A wartime slogan, particularly important in a dockland area, was 'Careless Talk Costs Lives', reminding everyone to beware of spies eavesdropping on conversations. For a road safety campaign in 1942, the slogan was amended to 'Careless Walk Costs Lives', pasted on the side of a tramcar.

Salford Victory Parade, Eccles Old Road, May 1945. The Police Band play as the British Legion contingent passes the Mayor. (Kemsley Newspaper)

A picture which is not what it seems. In the 1953 production of *Hobson's Choice*, several location shots were filmed in the Chapel Street area. Members of the Salford Police Band were persuaded to appear as the Salvation Army. (J. Dobson)

Section Twelve

PEOPLE AT WORK

In late Victorian times the number of people employed in the long-established trades of cotton spinning and weaving began to level off. Heavy engineering and electrical engineering assumed importance, and some new branches of the textile trade evolved. After the opening of the Ship Canal in 1894, more new industries were established, and the working population increased. Salford's central position in south-east Lancashire meant that many workers became involved in transport. By 1930, in terms of the numbers of people employed, transport headed the list, followed in order by metal workers and engineers, and those involved with textiles, wood, paper, and rubber. Subsequently, the decline of the staple industries had knock-on effects in reduced demand for machinery and associated services.

In post-war years, re-planning of the town has seen industry move out of Salford, as new factories have been located elsewhere. The population has fallen, and the work-force has been reduced. Once-extensive railway marshalling yards, factory land, and warehouses have disappeared under redevelopment schemes. However, there is still a wide range of industries in the city, and some former textile mills have been adapted to light engineering or the production of plastics.

An aerial view of Ordsall in 1932 shows the mixture of factories and terraced housing contained in a loop of the Ship Canal, formerly the River Irwell. Out of the picture to the left were the main terminal docks, a source of employment for many Ordsall residents, while off right, on the opposite bank, were the smaller Pomona Docks, used mainly by coastwise shipping. Factories occupied the land on the Salford side between

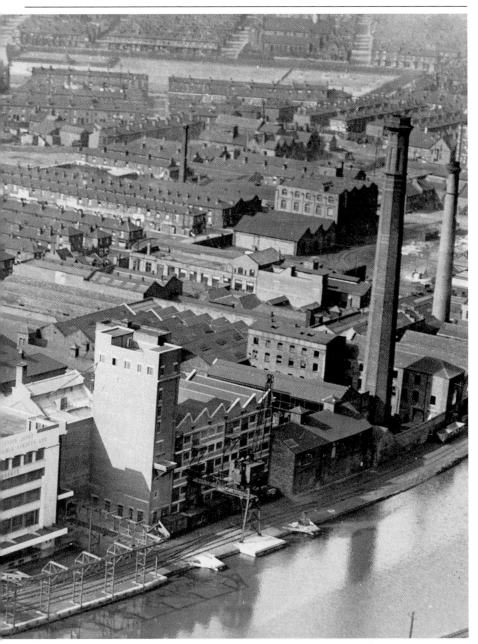

the Canal and Ordsall Lane. The Co-operative Society tea warehouse (centre) was newly built. On its wall was an illuminated sign in the shape of a teapot. The older factories to the right included Goodwin's Ivy Soap Works (later Colgate-Palmolive) and Richard Haworth's cotton mill. (NSR)

Lancashire's staple industry. A Lancashire Loom in the Tatton Weaving Shed of Richard Haworth's cotton mill on Ordsall Lane, 1963. Many girls leaving Ordsall schools gained employment at Haworth's, but the mill closed in the early 1970s. (SLHL)

Timber was a major import, and there was a large storage area by the end of Number 9 Dock, seen here before the First World War. Until the advent of stacker trucks, much of the work was done manually. Here, dockers negotiate plank walkways to stack timber.

Public transport brought a variety of associated tasks. A tramways employee, working in 1925 from a multi-purpose service vehicle, grinds out rail corrugations. The Frederick Smith cable drum gives its address as 'Salford, Manchester', a not uncommon practice. (SCT)

Leaf Square, Pendleton, *c.* 1905. Small businesses abounded. Frank Ellis specialised in providing stone blocks of all types, shapes and sizes. His storage yard was screened from Broad Street by tall hoardings.

Tram conductress, 1915. Because so many men had joined the forces, Salford Tramways appointed ladies to the traffic staff. Male workers opposed the arrangement on the grounds that the ladies were taking the jobs of men who had volunteered to fight. The idea of being supervised by female inspectors was even more firmly opposed, and so those ladies promoted had jurisdiction only over the conductresses. When the men returned from the army, the ladies were either dismissed or offered alternative employment in the cash or ticket offices.

Tramcar crew, Frederick Road Depot Yard, 1923. William Downsby (right) claimed to be the oldest motorman still in service. He had begun his career on horse-drawn trams in the 1870s, working for the Manchester Carriage & Tramways Company. The trolley-boy stands between him and the conductor.

Agecroft Power Station, 1930. To provide power for the electric tramways in 1901, a new coal-fired generating station (replacing a small 1895 unit) had been opened on Frederick Road, close to the bank of the Manchester, Bolton & Bury Canal. Critics alleged that it was far too large and of too great a capacity for the likely future demand. However, the rapid growth of industrial requirements led to a need for yet more generating capacity by 1914, and eventually to demands for an additional power station. The site chosen was on the Pendlebury bank of the Irwell at Agecroft, a convenient spot at which to receive bulk supplies of fuel from the nearby colliery, or by rail or canal. The new station was ready by 1924, and was subsequently expanded to provide many times its original output. In post-war years, its giant cooling towers became a local landmark. Both the colliery and the power station closed in 1994. (NSR)

Founded in 1875 and active for almost a century, the works of John Morris & Sons were situated close to Cross Lane. One unusual product of the textile industry was canvas fire hose, for which John Morris invented the instantaneous coupling. The brass coupling was fitted to the ends of fire hoses, offering instant means of connection to stand pipes, pumps, or other lengths. The firm grew to be a major supplier of fire-fighting equipment throughout the country. One of many useful devices was a hose-cleaning and re-winding machine (right), which squeezed out excess water, and brushed and cleaned the hose at the same time as winding it neatly.

Some trades took a long time to die. The sound of clogs on cobbled streets as workers set out for the early shift at the mill is said to have been the equivalent of a 'knocker-up' for many Lancashire children. James Critchley, a clogmaker and repairer, of Whit Lane, Salford, was still at work in 1950, and thought to be the last clogger in the area. (SLHL)

PEOPLE AT PLAY

Civic leaders of the Victorian period thought it was important for Salfordians to have open spaces for leisure pursuits, and consequently large areas of land were acquired for 'the enjoyment and recreation of the public'. In 1846 the Lark Hill Estate was purchased by public subscription and named Peel Park in honour of Sir Robert Peel. The estate mansion was transformed into a museum and library, which, in 1850, became the first unconditionally free municipal public library in the country.

Albert Park opened in 1877, Ordsall Park in 1879, Buile Hill in 1903, and assorted recreation grounds and playing fields followed. In the private sector, horse-racing on Kersal Moor dated from at least 1601, moving to Castle Irwell in 1847, five years after the River Irwell had staged its first regatta. In the early twentieth century, amateur clubs catered for all forms of sport.

The centre of indoor entertainment for many in Victorian times was the public house, from whose amateur concerts came some promising artistes, such as the musical comedy star Lily Elsie. The city also had several theatres, successful enough to attract major touring productions, but after 1912 the theatres were gradually outnumbered by cinemas. Today, the Salford Quays development has a new cinema complex, and offers water sports and fishing.

Peel Park, 1878. The building became a library, museum and art gallery, largely owing to the efforts of E.R. Langworthy, a former Mayor of the borough, and Joseph Brotherton, Salford's first MP.

Ordsall Hall, 1905. An ancient manor house, the Hall has had several owners. After a period as rectory for St Cyprian's Church (left, now demolished), the Hall was purchased by the Corporation, and opened as a museum in 1972. (TP)

Peel Park in the snow, *c.* 1904, viewed from the terrace behind the Art Gallery, and proving that the early postcard photographers occasionally braved the winter weather.

Winter sports in Broughton, 1907: skating on the pond in Clowes Park.

Seedley Park Bowling Green, *c.* 1905. Seedley Park is the lower portion of Buile Hill Park, where the former home of a Lord Mayor of Manchester was transformed into a Natural History Museum, now the Lancashire Mining Museum.

Buile Hill Park Lake, 1904. Up to and including the Second World War, all Salford parks had ornamental lakes, inhabited by ducks and swans. All except that in Light Oaks Park were inexplicably filled in after 1946.

Swinton Park was an extensive stretch of mixed farmland, with wide avenues of trees on the border between Salford and Swinton. Cut by the East Lancashire Road in 1933 and with a golf club occupying another portion, only a small area now remains as Oakwood Park.

Albert Park, 'The Swan's Retreat', 1920. Once an attractive park, giving pleasure to many, Albert Park is now a series of drab and featureless all-weather sports pitches, catering for only a few. (JLB)

A 1906 postcard entitled 'The Broughton Bowling Club' shows the members engaged in the indoor sport of billiards.

Members of the Salford Athletic & Cycling Club, several wearing passable imitations of Rugby Football jerseys, pose proudly for the camera in 1908. (G. Greenhalgh)

Taxi-cabs for the rich and/or winners, and tramcars for the losers or less wealthy, wait for punters to leave Castle Irwell Racecourse at the close of a race meeting about 1920.

Open-air parties, organised on a street-by-street basis, celebrated major events. This is Ouse Street, Weaste, decorated for the 1953 Coronation of Queen Elizabeth. (SLHL)

The Regent Theatre, Cross Lane, 1912. Opened in 1895, the structure also contained the Regent Assembly Rooms. Later renamed the Palace Theatre, it became mainly a cinema, but hosted occasional live theatre until destroyed by fire in 1956.

The Salford Royal Hippodrome, at the other end of Cross Lane, survived longer as a venue for live entertainment. Seen decorated for a royal visit, before the First World War, it was renamed the Windsor Theatre in 1956, and demolished in 1962. (SLHL)

The Tower Picture Palace, 1920s. On the corner of Great Clowes Street and Broughton Lane, it was a popular spot with the youth of the city. The building became a furniture store. (Barrett)

The Rialto Super Cinema, at the corner of Bury New Road and Great Cheetham Street, 1943. Exotically named, this picture palace was built in 1927, and remains in use, though it ceased to be a cinema in 1973.

The Bull's Head Hotel, Greengate, was an ancient tavern adapted from what had once been family houses in the older part of the city. Closed as an inn in 1930, the buildings were finally demolished some seven years later.

Cross Lane, pre-1912. The street was renowned for its large number of public houses. Close by the railway station were the London & North Western Hotel, the Station Hotel, and the Railway Hotel, the latter on the corner of West Albert Street.

RELIGIOUS & SOCIAL LIFE

As the population of the town grew, churches, chapels, and mission halls proliferated. In 1851 some 42 per cent of believers were Church of England, a similar number were Non-Conformist, and about 15 per cent were Roman Catholic. Religious and moral convictions exerted a powerful influence on local affairs. The first temperance society was founded in Salford, and used evangelical methods to increase membership. Self-help friendly societies, many connected with churches or chapels, offered assistance in times of sickness or bereavement to those who could afford weekly contributions.

The Co-operative Movement flourished, making good cheap food widely available. In the early twentieth century, Clothing Clubs, Christmas Clubs, and the like, allowed members to save small weekly sums until the time of need. The season for new clothes was Whitsuntide, when the annual Whit Walks provided an opportunity for members of the various churches to process through the streets with their banners and bands, demonstrating their commitment to their respective religions. For many children, it was also the time when new clothes had to be shown off to friends and relations, a tedious round relieved only by the tradition of coins being pushed into the wearer's pockets.

St Barnabas' Church, looking to Broughton, 1904. This was a medium-sized church, built on the gradient of Frederick Road. Ward & Goldstone's electrical engineering works later occupied the vacant land on the left.

Dock Mission, Mothers' Meeting, 1908. The Dock Mission was founded in a small hall in Ordsall, but moved to a former Wesleyan Chapel on New Park Road in 1915. For many dockland residents, it was the centre of social and religious life.

Whit Walks, Broad Street, Pendleton, 1913. Girls in their new dresses pass in the St George's Whit Friday procession. In the background is the outline of the Pendleton Public Baths on the corner of Frederick Road.

Ladies in the Whit Sunday procession of the combined Irlams O'Th'Height churches pass along Acresfield Road in 1912. A vacant plot off the picture to the right was later to become the site of Holy Angels C. of E. Church (see page 117).

Members of the Church Lads' Brigade, St Luke's C. of E. Church, Weaste, 1913. Many churches and missions preceded today's youth and social clubs in offering a range of leisure activities, including music, drama, dancing, and outdoor pursuits, for people of all ages. Participation usually, but not always, depended upon attendance at Sunday School or the evening service. Having a band associated with the church was an advantage on the occasion of the Whit Walks. (G. Greenhalgh)

Members of the 1st Weaste Scout Troop, July 1912.

The Independent Order of Rechabites was a world-wide teetotal society which originated in Salford in 1835. It was named after a tribe in the Book of Jeremiah which abstained from wine and lived in tents. These are children of the Stowell Church 'tent', 1907.

The Bishop of Hulme (Rt. Revd L.G. Hill) laying the foundation stone of Holy Angels Church, Irlams O'Th'Height, 1926. The church lay within an existing parish, but was a gift of the Heywood family, landowners in the area. (Stansfeld Parker)

The funerals of public employees who lost their lives in the course of duty were regarded as occasions for special mourning. The coffin of a fireman is carried on a Manchester Brigade tender, but the location is George Henry Street, Salford, and the date is probably about 1906.

The 1923 funeral cortège of a tram conductor, led by his General Manager. Joseph Mackay had been killed in an accident while escorting a blind passenger across the road. As a gesture of respect, all public transport in the city ceased for two minutes at 11 a.m. (A.P. King)

MOTOR BUSES

Although motor-driven charabancs had been in evidence for some years before the First World War, the electric tramway system had catered successfully for public transport needs, and it was not until 1920 that Salford purchased its first motor bus. The omnibus was not seen as a competitor to the tramway, but rather as a feeder to it. The first bus routes were arranged to run along roads which did not have a tramway, serving areas where it had not been thought worthwhile to construct track. However, growing competition from private omnibus companies forced the Corporation to run more buses, often in competition with its own trams.

With the wider adoption of the pneumatic tyre, the number of bus routes grew, competitors were bought out, and eventually, the motor bus proving a more flexible vehicle, the number of tram routes converted to bus operation increased. The last tram ran in 1947. The title of the undertaking was changed to Salford City Transport, with a new green and cream livery, in which guise municipal transport survived until absorbed into a Passenger Transport Board for the whole of Greater Manchester in 1969.

Salford's early double-deck buses were solid-tyred Leyland chassis, with bodies built by the English Electric Company, the latter firm having previously supplied tramcars. In 1923 there were 16 buses to 230 tramcars. (Leyland Motors)

Omnibuses lined up in Frederick Road Depot Yard in 1929 show a preponderance of single-deck vehicles, preferred by the undertaking after early experience with the open-top double-deckers.

In 1929 a second depot opened to house the growing omnibus fleet and to relieve the pressure on mixed accommodation at Frederick Road. A six-wheeled Karrier bus is parked over the inspection pits in the new Weaste Depot.

AEC bus 117 (RJ 3016) of 1934 had a metal-framed body, as patented by the Metropolitan Cammell Carriage & Wagon Company, a great advance on earlier styles. It remained in service for 15 years.

In the mid-1930s land alongside Victoria Bridge Street was purchased for conversion into a bus station. Work in progress in 1937 is viewed from the Manchester side of the Irwell, with Exchange Station and its approach to the right.

Victoria Bus Station, 1949, seen from the Exchange railway station approach, with vehicles sporting a variety of wartime and post-war liveries. The perimeter shelters were enclosed using vestibule doors from scrapped tramcars. (NSK)

Lancashire United Transport operated a number of joint routes into Salford. Most of their buses terminated in the gloomy Greengate arches beneath Exchange Station. Bus 53 (TJ 9380), a 1935 Leyland, waits to leave on service 12 in 1949. (NSK)

In 1951 Salford celebrated 50 years of municipal transport when this illuminated bus, CRJ 430, seen in Frederick Road Depot Yard, toured the city routes. It was one of the new 8-feet-wide Daimlers with Metro-Cammell body. (SCT)

Bus 162 (WRJ 162) Littleton Road, 1963. In the 1960s buses carried a more economical livery style, with the omission of two of the three cream bands. Defacement with external advertisements was still refused, however. (E. Gray)

Daimler TRJ 139 in the melting snow of Bolton Road, Irlams O'Th'Height, March 1970. Salford City Transport ceased to exist as a separate undertaking in 1969, but the familiar green livery graced the city streets for a little longer. (E. Gray)

In the 1960s the face of Salford changed irrevocably, not always for the better. Typifying much of the change is this scene in Taylorson Street, Ordsall, with a new tower block overshadowing the old corner shop and terraced houses. (Martin Maher)

Broad Street, 1992. In the 1970s and '80s road 'improvement' and motorway schemes cut great swathes through the heart of the city. In 1912 a police survey recorded that 3,400 vehicles passed this spot in an 8-hour period. Today that total would be in the region of 50,000. (E. Gray)

Acknowledgements

This collection of old photographs has been assembled over many years, and from a variety of sources. The author is indebted, as always, to the staff of the Salford Local History Library (Tim Ashworth, Tony Frankland, Sandra Hayton, and Patricia Nuttall), and to Andrew Cross, the Salford City Archivist. Friends and acquaintances have kindly produced or borrowed illustrations and relevant historical documents, including Brian Bennett (Monton), Roy Gillibrand (Whitefield), the Revd Stanley Horrocks (Broughton), John Howarth (Eccles), A.P. King (Salford), A.K. Kirby (Bramhall), Mrs Barbara Knott (Salford), Roy Mewha (Salford), T.J.B. Whiteley (Swinton), and members of the Salford Local History Society.

For permission to reproduce photographs, the author is indebted to J.R. Carter (Leigh), Godfrey Croughton (Kent), Martin Maher (Salford), the National Railway Museum (York), the Manchester Ship Canal Company, and the late W.A. Camwell (Birmingham) and R.B. Parr (Bingley). Illustrations are acknowledged individually where the photographer is known, and apologies are offered for any inadvertent omissions. Abbreviations used are:

SLHL	Salford Local History Library
MSCCo	Manchester Ship Canal Company
NRM	National Railway Museum
NSR	N.S. Roberts, Rochdale
JLB	J.L. Brown
TP	T. Pinder, Rochdale
EMC	Elsam, Mann & Cooper, Manchester
SCT	Salford City Transport
NSK	N.S. Kay, Manchester
RP	Real Photographs

For historical details used in the text and captions, the author has consulted the published works of Miss Evelyn Vigeon, J.A. Garrard, R.L. Greenall, V.I. Tomlinson, and the late A.T. Smith. Their researches are acknowledged with gratitude.

Finally, the author expresses his sincere thanks to his wife Kathleen for her constant support, tolerance, and encouragement.

BRITAIN IN OLD PHOTOGRAPHS

Scunthorpe, *D Taylor*
Skegness, *W Kime*
Around Skegness, *W Kime*

LONDON

Balham and Tooting, *P Loobey*
Crystal Palace, Penge & Anerley, *M Scott*
Greenwich and Woolwich, *K Clark*
Hackney: A Second Selection, *D Mander*
Lewisham and Deptford, *J Coulter*
Lewisham and Deptford: A Second Selection, *J Coulter*
Streatham, *P Loobey*
Around Whetstone and North Finchley, *J Heathfield*
Woolwich, *B Evans*

MONMOUTHSHIRE

Chepstow and the River Wye, *A Rainsbury*
Monmouth and the River Wye, *Monmouth Museum*

NORFOLK

Great Yarmouth, *M Teun*
Norwich, *M Colman*
Wymondham and Attleborough, *P Yaxley*

NORTHAMPTONSHIRE

Around Stony Stratford, *A Lambert*

NOTTINGHAMSHIRE

Arnold and Bestwood, *M Spick*
Arnold and Bestwood: A Second Selection, *M Spick*
Changing Face of Nottingham, *G Oldfield*
Mansfield, *Old Mansfield Society*
Around Newark, *T Warner*
Nottingham: 1944–1974, *D Whitworth*
Sherwood Forest, *D Ottewell*
Victorian Nottingham, *M Payne*

OXFORDSHIRE

Around Abingdon, *P Horn*
Banburyshire, *M Barnett & S Gosling*
Burford, *A Jewell*
Around Didcot and the Hagbournes, *B Lingham*
Garsington, *M Gunther*
Around Henley-on-Thames, *S Ellis*
Oxford: The University, *J Rhodes*
Thame to Watlington, *N Hood*
Around Wallingford, *D Beasley*
Witney, *T Worley*
Around Witney, *C Mitchell*
Witney District, *T Worley*
Around Woodstock, *J Bond*

POWYS

Brecon, *Brecknock Museum*
Welshpool, *E Bredsdorff*

SHROPSHIRE

Shrewsbury, *D Trumper*
Whitchurch to Market Drayton, *M Morris*

SOMERSET

Bath, *J Hudson*
Bridgwater and the River Parrett, *R Fitzhugh*
Bristol, *D Moorcroft & N Campbell-Sharp*
Changing Face of Keynsham,
  B Lowe & M Whitehead

Chard and Ilminster, *G Gosling & F Huddy*
Crewkerne and the Ham Stone Villages,
  G Gosling & F Huddy
Around Keynsham and Saltford, *B Lowe & T Brown*
Midsomer Norton and Radstock, *C Howell*
Somerton, Ilchester and Langport, *G Gosling & F Huddy*
Taunton, *N Chipchase*
Around Taunton, *N Chipchase*
Wells, *C Howell*
Weston-Super-Mare, *S Poole*
Around Weston-Super-Mare, *S Poole*
West Somerset Villages, *K Houghton & L Thomas*

STAFFORDSHIRE

Aldridge, *J Farrow*
Bilston, *E Rees*
Black Country Transport: Aviation, *A Brew*
Around Burton upon Trent, *G Sowerby & R Farman*
Bushbury, *A Chatwin, M Mills & E Rees*
Around Cannock, *M Mills & S Belcher*
Around Leek, *R Poole*
Lichfield, *H Clayton & K Simmons*
Around Pattingham and Wombourne, *M Griffiths,*
  P Leigh & M Mills
Around Rugeley, *T Randall & J Anslow*
Smethwick, *J Maddison*
Stafford, *J Anslow & T Randall*
Around Stafford, *J Anslow & T Randall*
Stoke-on-Trent, *I Lawley*
Around Tamworth, *R Sulima*
Around Tettenhall and Codsall, *M Mills*
Tipton, Wednesbury and Darlaston, *R Pearson*
Walsall, *D Gilbert & M Lewis*
Wednesbury, *I Bott*
West Bromwich, *R Pearson*

SUFFOLK

Ipswich: A Second Selection, *D Kindred*
Around Ipswich, *D Kindred*
Around Mildenhall, *C Dring*
Southwold to Aldeburgh, *H Phelps*
Around Woodbridge, *H Phelps*

SURREY

Cheam and Belmont, *P Berry*
Croydon, *S Bligh*
Dorking and District, *K Harding*
Around Dorking, *A Jackson*
Around Epsom, *P Berry*
Farnham: A Second Selection, *J Parratt*
Around Haslemere and Hindhead, *T Winter & G Collyer*
Richmond, *Richmond Local History Society*
Sutton, *P Berry*

SUSSEX

Arundel and the Arun Valley, *J Godfrey*
Bishopstone and Seaford, *P Pople & P Berry*
Brighton and Hove, *J Middleton*
Brighton and Hove: A Second Selection, *J Middleton*
Around Crawley, *M Goldsmith*
Hastings, *P Haines*
Hastings: A Second Selection, *P Haines*
Around Haywards Heath, *J Middleton*
Around Heathfield, *A Gillet & B Russell*
Around Heathfield: A Second Selection,
  A Gillet & B Russell
High Weald, *B Harwood*
High Weald: A Second Selection, *B Harwood*
Horsham and District, *T Wales*

Lewes, *J Middleton*
RAF Tangmere, *A Saunders*
Around Rye, *A Dickinson*
Around Worthing, *S White*

WARWICKSHIRE

Along the Avon from Stratford to Tewkesbury, *J Jeremiah*
Bedworth, *J Burton*
Coventry, *D McGrory*
Around Coventry, *D McGrory*
Nuneaton, *S Clews & S Vaughan*
Around Royal Leamington Spa, *J Cameron*
Around Royal Leamington Spa: A Second Selection,
  J Cameron
Around Warwick, *R Booth*

WESTMORLAND

Eden Valley, *J Marsh*
Kendal, *M & P Duff*
South Westmorland Villages, *J Marsh*
Westmorland Lakes, *J Marsh*

WILTSHIRE

Around Amesbury, *P Daniels*
Chippenham and Lacock, *A Wilson & M Wilson*
Around Corsham and Box, *A Wilson & M Wilson*
Around Devizes, *D Buxton*
Around Highworth, *G Tanner*
Around Highworth and Faringdon, *G Tanner*
Around Malmesbury, *A Wilson*
Marlborough: A Second Selection, *P Colman*
Around Melksham,
  Melksham and District Historical Association
Nadder Valley, *R. Sawyer*
Salisbury, *P Saunders*
Salisbury: A Second Selection, *P Daniels*
Salisbury: A Third Selection, *P Daniels*
Around Salisbury, *P Daniels*
Swindon: A Third Selection, *The Swindon Society*
Swindon: A Fourth Selection, *The Swindon Society*
Trowbridge, *M Marshman*
Around Wilton, *P Daniels*
Around Wootton Bassett, Cricklade and Purton, *T Sharp*

WORCESTERSHIRE

Evesham to Bredon, *F Archer*
Around Malvern, *K Smith*
Around Pershore, *M Dowty*
Redditch and the Needle District, *R Saunders*
Redditch: A Second Selection, *R Saunders*
Around Tenbury Wells, *D Green*
Worcester, *M Dowty*
Around Worcester, *R Jones*
Worcester in a Day, *M Dowty*
Worcestershire at Work, *R Jones*

YORKSHIRE

Huddersfield: A Second Selection, *H Wheeler*
Huddersfield: A Third Selection, *H Wheeler*
Leeds Road and Rail, *R Vickers*
Pontefract, *R van Riel*
Scarborough, *D Coggins*
Scarborough's War Years, *R Percy*
Skipton and the Dales, *Friends of the Craven Museum*
Around Skipton-in-Craven, *Friends of the Craven Museum*
Yorkshire Wolds, *I & M Sumner*